PAROS ISLAND TRA

2023

The Simple Guide to Eventful Paros Travel Experiences: Where to Stay, Money-Saving Tips, Transportation, Cuisine, Recommended Activities, Top Hotels, and More

Vickie Davis

INTRODUCTION

HISTORY ABOUT PAROS

GEOGRAPHY AND CLIMATE OF PAROS

PAROS HOW TO GET AROUND

HOW TO SAVE MONEY AND BUDGET ON PAROS VISIT

CHAPTER 1

GREECE TRAVEL TIPS FOR BEGINNERS: GUIDANCE AND DETAILS FOR FIRST-TIME TRAVELERS

BOOKING HOTELS, FLIGHTS, FERRIES, & TOURS

GREEK CURRENCY AND TIPPING IN GREECE

COMMON GREEK WORDS & PHRASES

DRESS CODE IN GREECE

Dress Code in Paros

DRIVING IN GREECE

TAXIS AND UBER IN GREECE

SMOKING IN GREECE

DRINKING IN GREECE

TIPS AND ADVICE FOR THE BEST PLACES TO STAY IN PAROS

Best places to stay in Paros

CHAPTER 2

BEST PLACES TO STAY IN PAROS
NAOUSSA
The Best Hotels in Naoussa
PARIKIA
The best places to stay in Parikia include:
LIVADIA
Livadia's Top Hotels
PARASPOROS BEACH
The Best Hotels in Parasporos Beach
Antiparos
Top Hotels in Antiparos
CHRISSI AKTI BEACH AND NEA CHRISSI AKTI BEACH
The Best Hotel at Chrissi Akti Beach
The Best Hotel on Nea Chrissi Akti Beach.
LEFKES
The Best Hotels in Lefkes
FISHING VILLAGES
The Best Hotels in Piso Livadi
The Best Hotels in Aliki
The Best Hotels in Ambelas
The Best Hotels in Drios

CHAPTER 3

WHICH IS BETTER PAROS OR NAXOS
WHICH IS BETTER PAROS OR MYKONOS
WHICH IS BETTER PAROS OR MILOS
WHICH IS BETTER PAROS OR SANTORINI?

CHAPTER 4

PAROS WEATHER BY MONTH

CHAPTER 5

PACOS WITHOUT CAR

CHAPTER 6

CUISINE

CHAPTER 7

TIPS AND RECOMMENDATIONS FOR PAROS HOTELS
TOP HOTELS
THE SAINT ANDREA SEASIDE RESORT
THE POSEIDON OF PAROS HOTEL & SPA
THE PARILIO IS AN ALL-SUITE LUXURY HOTEL
THE HOTEL SENIA IS A GORGEOUS LUXURY HOTEL
THE PALIOMYLOS SPA HOTEL IS AN UPSCALE HOTEL
LILLY RESIDENCE
KANALE'S ROOMS AND SUITES
ASTIR OF PAROS
MINOIS VILLAGE BOUTIQUE SUITES & SPA
STELIA MARE BOUTIQUE HOTEL
KALLISTI ROOMS AND APARTMENTS
ANNA PLATANOU SUITES
KALYPSO HOTEL
MR. AND MRS. WHITE PAROS
PAROSLAND HOTEL
ARGONAUTA HOTEL
PENSION SOFIA

VILLA ISABELLA

BEACHES IN PAROS

FAMILY-FRIENDLY HOTELS IN PAROS

CHAPTER 8

PAROS FOR KIDS

CHAPTER 9

ACTIVITIES AND ATTRACTIONS AVAILABLE IN PAROS

TOP TWO TOURS TO ENJOY IN PAROS

THE TOP THINGS TO DO IN PAROS

PAROS PARK

KOLYMBITHRES BEACH

THE CHURCH OF PANAGIA EKATONTAPILIANI

THE CHARMING VILLAGE OF NAOUSSA

PARIKIA

KALOGEROS BEACH

NAXOS

NAOUSSA'S OLD PORT

LEFKES

MORAITIS WINERY

WINDSURFING AND KITESURFING:

ANTIPAROS DAY TRIP:

SANTA MARIA BEACH:

FISHING COMMUNITIES:

PAROS ARCHAEOLOGICAL MUSEUM:

PAROS NIGHTLIFE:

PAROS DINING:

BUTTERFLIES VALLEY:

CHAPTER 10

ANSWERS TO FREQUENTLY ASKED QUESTIONS

WHERE IS PAROS LOCATED?

HOW BIG IS PAROS?

WHAT IS THE HISTORY OF PAROS?

WHEN IS THE BEST TIME TO VISIT PAROS

HOW CAN YOU GET TO PAROS?

WHAT ARE THE MAIN TOWNS IN PAROS?

IS PAROS EXPENSIVE?

WHY TRAVEL TO PAROS?

IS PAROS A PARTY ISLAND?

CAN YOU FLY TO PAROS FROM UK

WHAT ARE SOME OF THE TOP BEACHES IN PAROS?

HOW MANY DAYS SHOULD I SPEND IN PAROS?

HOW CAN I GET AROUND PAROS?

HOW DO I GET TO ANTIPAROS?

CURRENCY USED IN PAROS?

IS PAROS GOOD FOR FAMILIES

GLOSSARY

INTRODUCTION

I had always heard about the stunning beauty of the Greek Cyclades islands, but I never imagined I would find myself on the island of Paros.

My previous trips to the Cyclades had been to the much more famous and popular islands of Mykonos and Santorini. However, when a friend suggested we explore Paros, I was curious to discover this lesser-known island.

Arriving at the port of Parikia, the main town of Paros, I was immediately struck by the island's charm.

The white-washed houses, colorful flowers, and narrow streets made me feel like I had stepped back in time.

The town was lively, but not overly crowded, which was a welcome change from the hustle and bustle of Mykonos.

We checked into our hotel, which was conveniently located in the heart of Parikia, and then headed to the beach. We had heard that Paros had some of the best beaches in the Cyclades, and we were not disappointed.

The crystal-clear waters and white sandy beaches were just as beautiful as the more famous beaches of Mykonos, but without the crowds.

As we explored the island, we discovered that Paros had a lot to offer. From picturesque villages, like Naoussa, to ancient monuments, like the Temple of Apollo, there was always something new to see and experience.

The island's rich history and culture were evident in every corner.

But what convinced me that Paros was better than the more famous Cyclades islands was the people.

The locals were friendly and welcoming, and we felt like we were part of the community.

It was a refreshing change from the impersonal vibe of Mykonos, where the locals often seemed jaded by the constant stream of tourists.

On our last night in Paros, we dined at a local taverna, where we savored fresh seafood and delicious Greek wine.

As we watched the sunset over the harbor, I knew that Paros had captured my heart. It was a magical place, where tradition and beauty coexisted in perfect harmony.

In the end, it was the people, the history, and the natural beauty of Paros that convinced me that it was better than the more famous Cyclades islands.

It's a hidden gem that deserves to be explored and appreciated by all those who love the magic of Greece.

History about Paros

Paros is a small, beautiful island in the Cyclades, part of the large archipelago that is known as the "Greek Islands". Located in the Aegean Sea, it lies to the southwest of the island of Mykonos and to the north of Naxos and the other Cyclades islands.

The island is known for its villages, harbors, and crystal-clear water. Lush green hills, scattered with dry stonewall houses dominated by many small windmills and ancient churches are signs that make Paros one of the most idyllic holiday spots in Greece.

Originally known as Peparithos, Paros became an important island in Greek history due to its position in the maritime trade routes of the Mediterranean.

An important port-of-call and trading center during the Mycenaean period, it was the birthplace of the poet and scholar Sappho, the most famous ancient female poet and the symbol of lyricism throughout the centuries.

The ancient city of Paros was a center of Literature, Arts, and Sciences, and it was home to a formidable School of Philosophy, whose members included Protagoras and Democritus.

Paros was also an important naval power during the days of Ancient Greece. The island was able to maintain an independent navy during the first part of the 5th century BC and this allowed it to take part in many seafaring, and naval battles. As a reward for its steadfast loyalty during the Persian Wars, it was recognized by the Athenians in 476 BC, granting it the coveted status of autonomous democracy.

The island was also one of the few areas of refuge for the persecuted and enslaved Jews during the Greco-Roman period. As such, the island became known for its diverse cultural heritage and the hospitality of its people. It was this passion for heritage and hospitality that later made Paros an important center for the cultivation and devotion to a culture that is still evident today.

Paros has been an important trading partner for many countries throughout its long recorded history.

It is believed that it was explored by the Phoenicians during the ninth century BC and colonized by the Ionians in the seventh century BC. Later, Paros was the birthplace of a major wheat-exporting industry, based primarily in the ports of Naousa and Parikia, which continued to be a source of agricultural wealth until the 18th century.

In modern times, Paros's incredible beauty and relative peace have made it a haven for artists, writers, and celebrities looking for a serene place to work and relax. Its stunning beaches and azure waters have also made it an attractive destination for tourists seeking some sun and fun. Kolymbithres, a unique rock formation near Naousa, is an especially popular destination.

Other popular attractions include the 12th-century Byzantine Church of Ekatontapiliani and its surrounding Byzantine Museum, the enchanting hilltop village of Prodromos, and a large number of ancient ruins scattered across the island.

Due to its strategic location, gorgeous beaches, and hospitable people, Paros is the perfect place to explore and relax. Its long and iconic history puts the island in a class of its own, and its archaeological relics, cultural heritage, and natural beauty guarantee a unique island-hopping experience. With plenty of traditional seafood restaurants, lively nightlife, and diverse activities to choose from, Paros is sure to be one of the most unforgettable and extraordinary vacation destinations of your   life.

Geography and Climate of Paros

The physical geography of Paros consists of mountains, cliffs, and large plains.

The island is mainly composed of limestone, marble, and volcanic soil, with some areas being rich in iron ore, oil residue, and clay.

Paros is known for its breathtaking views of the sea and is surrounded by a protective and tranquil atmosphere. There are many small islands in the surrounding area, and it is easy to find boat or ferry rides to nearby destinations such as Naxos, Mykonos, and Santorini.

Paros is known for its subtropical Mediterranean climate and typically experiences mild winters and hot summers, with July and August being the hottest months. Rainfall is quite regular throughout the year and most months receive an average of 3 inches.

The temperatures average 27°C during the summer and 12°C during the winter, making Paros a great destination for beachgoers, hikers, and nature lovers alike.

The crystal clear waters of Paros provide an excellent opportunity for swimming, snorkeling, and diving, while the rocky coastline is great for exploring.

Various sports are also available on the island, such as windsurfing and kitesurfing, or visiting the many historical sites, churches, and archaeological ruins that dot the landscape.

The culture of Paros is unique and locals are proud of their long-held traditions.

Paros is well known for its delicious and traditional cuisine which includes a variety of Greek dishes such as moussaka, souvlaki, and dolmas.

A variety of festivals and events are held throughout the year, such as the Paros Music Festival, the International Archaeological Film Festival, and the annual swimming competition.

Paros How to Get Around

Paros is a small island in Greece, and there are several ways to get around:

On foot: Paros is a small island, and many of its attractions can be explored on foot. Walking is a great way to explore the island, and it allows you to discover hidden gems that you might miss otherwise.

By bike: Biking is a popular way to get around Paros, and there are several bike rental shops on the island. Biking is a great way to explore the island at your own pace and enjoy the beautiful scenery.

By car: Hiring a car is an excellent option if you want to explore the island at your own pace. There are several car rental companies on the island, and prices are generally reasonable.

By bus: Paros has a good bus network, which is cheap and reliable. The buses run frequently, and they can take you to all the major towns and beaches on the island.

By taxi: Taxis in Paros can be expensive, but they are a good option if you want to get around quickly and comfortably. There are several taxi companies on the island, and you can also hail a taxi on the street.

By boat: Paros is a popular island-hopping destination, and several boats connect it to other islands in the Cyclades. Several boat tours allow you to explore the island from the sea.

Using these different modes of transportation, you can easily get around Paros and explore all the island offers.

How to Save Money and Budget on Paros Visit

Paros is a beautiful island in Greece with a lot of things to offer to visitors, but it's important to keep your budget in check.

Here are some tips on how to save money and budget for your Paros visit:

Choose the right time to visit: The peak tourist season in Paros is from June to August, and during this time, prices for accommodation, food, and activities are at their highest.

To save money, consider visiting during the shoulder season (May, September, or October) when prices are lower and the weather is still pleasant.

Book in advance: Booking your accommodation, flights, and activities in advance can help you save money, as you may be able to take advantage of early-bird discounts.

Stay-in-budget accommodation: Paros has various accommodation options to suit different budgets, including hostels, guesthouses, and apartments. Consider staying in a budget-friendly option to save money.

Eat like a local: Paros has many restaurants and tavernas serving traditional Greek cuisine, which can be quite expensive.

To save money, eat like a local by visiting the island's bakeries, supermarkets, and street food vendors.

Use public transport: Taxis in Paros can be expensive, so consider using public transport instead.

The island has a good bus network, which is cheap and reliable.

Explore the island on foot: Paros is a small island, and many of its attractions can be explored on foot. Consider walking or cycling instead of hiring a car or taking a taxi.

Take advantage of free activities: Paros has many free activities and attractions, such as the beaches, the Old Town, and the churches.

Take advantage of these to save money on your trip.

By following these tips, you can save money and budget for your Paros visit, without compromising on the quality of your trip.

CHAPTER 1

Greece Travel Tips for Beginners: Guidance and Details for First-Time Travelers

Booking Hotels, Flights, Ferries, & Tours

To ensure availability, I usually book flights 6 to 9 months in advance. Waiting longer might result in limited availability.

Conversely, booking too early may not include all flights. For hotels, I recommend booking 4 to 6 months ahead, as prices tend to rise and rooms become scarce closer to the travel date. Most hotels make rooms available for booking up to 9 months in advance. To secure preferred tours, I suggest booking 3 to 5 months ahead.

Finally, ferry tickets should be the last to book, with popular routes like Athens to Santorini or Mykonos to Santorini selling out quickly, while large car ferries rarely sell out. Booking online is recommended for convenience.

Greek Currency and Tipping In Greece

In Greece, the official currency is the euro (€), which is accepted in most major shops and restaurants.

However, some places may require a minimum purchase to use credit cards.

ATMs are widely available in big cities like Athens and most Greek towns and beaches.

It's advisable to carry cash for small purchases like bus fares and snacks. Bargaining is not expected in most Greek shops, as they typically have fixed prices.

While tipping in Greek restaurants is not mandatory, it is a kind gesture.

Instead of a percentage of the bill, tipping is usually a few euros left on the table as a token of appreciation for good service or rounding up the total.

The hotel cleaning staff also appreciate a small tip left in the room, with a suggested amount of 1-2 euros per night stayed.

Common Greek Words & Phrases

Hello/Goodbye: Γειά σας (Yia sas) - YEA-sahs

Good morning: Καλημέρα (Kaliméra) - kah-lee-MEH-rah

Good afternoon/evening: Καλησπέρα (Kalispéra) - kah-lee-SPARE-ah

Thank you: Ευχαριστώ (Efcharistó) - eff-har-ee-STO

Thank you very much: Ευχαριστώ πολύ (Efcharistó polý) - eff-har-ee-STO po-LEE

Please/you're welcome: Παρακαλώ (Parakaló) - par-ah-kah-LO

Yes: Ναι (Ne) - neh

No: Όχι (Ochi) - O-hee

I don't understand: Δεν καταλαβαίνω (Den katalavaíno) - then kah-tah-lah-VEH-no

Goodbye: (literally "be happy"): Χαιρετε (Chaírete) - HARE-eh-teh

Goodnight: Καληνύχτα (Kalinychta) - kah-lee-NEE-htah

• How are you?: Ti káneis? (tee KAH-nees?)

• I'm fine, thanks: Kala, efcharistó (kah-lah, eff-har-ee-STO)

• What's your name?: Pos se lene? (pohs seh LEH-neh?)

• My name is...: Me lene... (meh LEH-neh...)

• Where is...?: Pu einai...? (poo EH-neh?)

• Excuse me: Signómi (see-GNOH-mee)

• Sorry: Sygnómi (seeg-NOH-mee)

• It's okay: Íne kála (EE-neh KAH-lah)

• I don't speak Greek: Den miláo elliniká (then mee-LAH-oh eh-lee-nee-KAH)

• Do you speak English?: Milás angliká? (MEE-lahs ahn-GLEE-kah?)

• Help!: Voítheia! (voh-THEE-ah!)

• Where is the bathroom?: Pu einai i toualéta? (poo EH-neh ee too-ah-LEH-tah?)

• One beer, please: Mia mpíra, parakaló (MEE-ah BEE-rah, pah-rah-kah-LOH)

• How much does it cost?: Pósó káni aftó? (POH-soh KAH-nee AHF-toh?)

• I love you: S' agapó (S' ah-GAH-poh

Dress Code in Greece

The appropriate attire in Greece depends on the location. Beachwear is appropriate for the beach, but it should not be worn when wandering around town.

Although locals seldom do it, topless sunbathing is common in beach clubs.

The dress code in most restaurants is relatively casual, but it is advisable to wear well-maintained t-shirts and shorts.

Some monasteries and churches have dress code rules that require women to wear skirts and forbid bare shoulders or knees.

Cover garments are typically provided for those who need them.

Dress Code in Paros

The dress code for travelers in Paros is generally casual and comfortable, especially during the hot summer months.

When visiting the beaches or engaging in outdoor activities, it's common to wear swimsuits, shorts, and t-shirts.

However, it's important to note that while beachwear is acceptable on beaches, it may not be appropriate in other public areas such as shops, restaurants, or churches.

For visiting religious sites or more formal occasions, it's recommended to dress more modestly.

This means wearing clothing that covers the shoulders and knees, such as dresses, skirts, or long pants.

It's also worth noting that many restaurants and bars in Paros have a relaxed dress code, but some may require more elegant attire for dinner or evening events.

In general, it's always a good idea to bring comfortable shoes, a hat, sunglasses, and sunscreen to protect yourself from the strong Greek sun.

Driving In Greece

In Greece, cars drive on the right side of the road with the steering wheel on the left.

Highways and primary roads in Greece have good conditions and clear signage.

An International driver's Permit is required for foreign drivers in Greece. It is a good idea to rent a car in advance, particularly if you need an automatic transmission.

RentalCars.com is a simple and effective website for renting cars in Greece.

Taxis and Uber in Greece

Taxi cabs in Greece have a maximum limit of four passengers per vehicle, and sharing cabs is typical. It is appropriate to hail a taxi with passengers already in it, and each person pays their own fare.

If you do not want to be joined by strangers during your cab ride, tell the driver in advance, and they must comply with the law.

Taxis outside of significant cities are often picked up at designated taxi stands, and if you try to hail a taxi in close proximity to a designated taxi stand, they will direct you to the stand.

Tipping is not expected, but a few euros or rounding up the fare is appreciated.

While Uber is present in Greece, Beat is the most commonly used and reliable ride-share app.

Welcome Pickups car service is a suitable pre-booked alternative to a taxi for port and airport transfers in Greece.

The price is comparable to that of a cab, larger vehicles are available for groups of more than four, and child car seats are available upon request.

Smoking in Greece

Although cigarette smoking is widespread in Greece, it is generally forbidden indoors.

Some restaurants overlook this rule.

Greek hotels do not provide smoking rooms, but smoking is permitted on a private or shared terrace or in any of the outdoor common areas.

It is typical for individuals to smoke at outdoor tables in Greek restaurants, and smoke from outside sometimes blows indoors.

Drinking in Greece

In Greece, the legal drinking age is 16. It is uncommon for Greeks to drink on an empty stomach, and being intoxicated in public is discouraged.

After a meal, some restaurants may provide a complimentary digestif.

Tips and Advice for the Best Places to Stay in Paros

• For a mix of walkability, dining, nightlife, shopping, and good beach access, stay in Parikia or Naoussa.

• For an idyllic beach escape at a slow pace, stay in Antiparos or Chrissi Akti.

• To explore natural wonders, stay in Livadia.

• For authentic Greek hospitality, wonderful food, and great beaches, stay in a fishing village - Piso Livadi, Aliki, or Drios.

• Best website for booking hotels in Paros is **Booking.com**.

Best places to stay in Paros

Best hotels:

- ✓ Poseidon of Paros Hotel & Spa
- ✓ Saint Andrea Seaside Resort
- ✓ Parilio

Best hotels for families:

- ✓ Poseidon of Paros Hotel & Spa
- ✓ Saint Andrea Seaside Resort
- ✓ Astir of Paros.

Best cheap hotels:

- ✓ Margarita Studios
- ✓ Villa Isabella Studios and Suites
- ✓ Pension Sofia.

Best honeymoon hotels:

- ✓ Parilio
- ✓ Hotel Senia
- ✓ Lilly Residence - Adults Only

Best areas for most travelers:

For most travelers, **Parikia** and **Naoussa** are the best places to stay in Paros because they have easy access to beautiful beaches, various dining options, fun nightlife, and boutique shopping.

These areas offer a wide range of accommodation options to fit all budgets.

Best sightseeing places:

Parikia, Naoussa, and Livadia are the best areas for sightseeing. Parikia has a Byzantine church, Frankish castle ruins, an archaeological museum, and sunset views. Naoussa has the Old Port, Venetian castle ruins, and a winery. Livadia is close to Kolymbithres Beach and Paros Park.

Best places for living like a local:

Piso Livadi, Ambelas, Aliki, and Drios are the best places to experience local life.

These picturesque fishing villages have small marinas, authentic tavernas serving fresh seafood, and beautiful beaches. Piso Livadi is the busiest of the four with more beach clubs, while Ambelas and Aliki are suitable for families, and Drios is quieter except during August.

Best places for a beach vacation:

.Chrissi Akti (Golden Beach) is an excellent place for a beach vacation.

It has a long stretch of soft sand, turquoise water, beach clubs, a dive center, and a water sports center. Alternatively, Antiparos, a laid-back island visible from Paros, has several idyllic sandy beaches.

CHAPTER 2

Best places to stay in Paros

Naoussa

Naoussa, a cosmopolitan village, is more modern than Parikia but is just as charming. It is situated in a natural bay at the north end of the island with fishing boats anchored, and a Venetian castle from the 12th century that is partially sunken in the Old Port.

A water taxi from the old port connects Naoussa to Kolymbithres Beach, famous for its moon-like rock formations, Monastiri Beach, which is family-friendly and part of Paros Park, and Laggeri Beach, a popular clothing-optional beach.

Numerous picturesque seafood restaurants and cocktail bars line the waterfront. Moving inland, you will find the typical Cycladic maze of pedestrian streets, teeming with vibrant bougainvillea, boutiques, churches, and a winery.

Dining, nightlife, and lodging here tend to be trendier and more luxurious than in Parikia, although many casual choices are still available.

The Best Hotels in Naoussa

- ✓ Hotel Senia
- ✓ Paliomylos Spa Hotel
- ✓ Lilly Residence – Adults Only
- ✓ Kanale's Rooms & Suites
- ✓ Stelia Mare Boutique Hotel
- ✓ Kallisti Rooms & Apartments

Parikia

Parikia is the main port town and the capital of Paros Island. It is located on the western coast of the island and is the first stop for many visitors arriving by ferry.

The town is a hub of activity and is known for its lively atmosphere, charming alleys, and ancient landmarks.

One of the top attractions in Parikia is the Panagia Ekatontapiliani, also known as the Church of 100 Doors.

This Byzantine church dates back to the 4th century and is one of the oldest and most important religious sites in Greece.

The church is renowned for its stunning mosaics, intricate frescoes, and unique architecture.

The old town of Parikia is another must-see attraction. It is a maze of narrow streets, alleys, and squares that are lined with traditional white-washed houses adorned with colorful flowers.

The town is home to a variety of shops, cafes, and restaurants, making it a great place to wander and explore.

Parikia also has some of the best beaches on the island, including Livadia Beach, which is the closest to the town and is perfect for families with children.

The beach has a long stretch of golden sand and clear blue waters, as well as many beach bars, cafes, and restaurants.

Another popular beach in Parikia is Krios Beach, which is located on the other side of the bay and is known for its crystal-clear waters and magnificent views of the town and the sunset.

Parikia has a wide range of accommodation options to suit all budgets, including luxury hotels, villas, and apartments, as well as more affordable guesthouses and hostels.

In terms of activities, Parikia has something for everyone. For history buffs, the Archaeological Museum of Paros is a must-visit attraction, which displays a wide range of ancient artifacts and relics from the island's rich history.

Outdoor enthusiasts will enjoy exploring the hiking trails of Paros, which offer stunning views of the coastline and the surrounding countryside.

Overall, Parikia is a charming town that offers visitors a perfect blend of ancient history, stunning natural beauty, and modern comforts.

Whether you're looking for a romantic getaway or a family vacation, Parikia has something to offer for everyone.

The best places to stay in Parikia include:

- ✓ Argonauta Hotel
- ✓ Pension Sofia
- ✓ Apollon Boutique Hotel

Livadia

Livadia, which should not be mistaken for Livadia Beach in Parikia, is a deluxe resort area situated between Naoussa village and Kolymbithres Beach.

Despite having been the location of a Mycenaean acropolis in the past, it is now dominated by high-end hotels and villas.

Whether you are seeking a romantic retreat or a family vacation, Livadia is an excellent choice, offering peaceful and calm evenings with convenient access to Naoussa's dining, shopping, and nightlife, as well as Kolymbithres Beach's impressive granite rock formations and Paros Park's sandy beaches and hiking trails.

Since there are no restaurants or markets in the vicinity, it is recommended that you stay at a hotel with a shuttle service to Naoussa and Kolymbithres (many are available) or rent a car.

Livadia's Top Hotels

- ✓ Parilio
- ✓ Blue Mare Villas
- ✓ Saint Andrea Seaside Resort
- ✓ Astir of Paros
- ✓ Angels Villas

Parasporos Beach

Parasporos Beach is a stunning crescent-shaped beach on the southwestern coast of the Greek island of Paros.

The beach boasts clear, turquoise waters, soft golden sand, and an unspoiled natural setting, making it a popular destination for tourists and locals alike.

Parasporos Beach is easily accessible, with a paved road leading directly to the shore, making it a great choice for families with young children or those with mobility concerns.

The beach has all the amenities you would expect, including sun loungers and umbrellas, showers, and changing rooms.

There are also several beach bars and restaurants in the area, offering refreshments and local cuisine.

The waters at Parasporos Beach are perfect for swimming and snorkeling, with a variety of sea life to be seen in the clear, shallow waters.

Visitors can also explore the nearby caves and coves, and take a leisurely stroll along the scenic walking paths that wind through the surrounding hills and cliffs.

For those looking to stay in the area, there are several accommodation options available, from hotels and resorts to self-catering apartments and villas.

Parasporos Beach is conveniently located near the town of Parikia, which offers a range of shops, restaurants, and nightlife.

Overall, Parasporos Beach is a must-visit destination for anyone traveling to Paros. Its stunning natural setting, clear waters, and range of activities make it a perfect spot for families, couples, and solo travelers alike.

Whether you're looking for a relaxing day on the beach or an adventure exploring the surrounding area, Parasporos Beach has something for everyone.

The Best Hotels in Parasporos Beach

- ✓ Minois Village Boutique Suites & Spa
- ✓ Yria Island Boutique Hotel & Spa

Antiparos

Antiparos is a small island located just a short boat ride away from the larger island of Paros, in the Cyclades archipelago of Greece.

Although it is less well-known than Paros, Antiparos has much to offer visitors, from beautiful beaches and crystal-clear waters to charming traditional villages and ancient archaeological sites.

One of the most popular attractions on Antiparos is the Cave of Antiparos, a vast underground cavern with stunning stalactites and stalagmites that are believed to be around 45 million years old.

Visitors can take a guided tour of the cave, which is accessed by a series of steep steps that lead down into the darkness.

The temperature inside the cave remains constant year-round, making it a great escape from the heat of the Greek summer.

Another must-see attraction on Antiparos is the Venetian Castle, which was built in the 15th century to protect the island from marauding pirates.

The castle is located at the highest point on the island and offers incredible views of the surrounding sea and countryside.

Visitors can explore the castle's ramparts, towers, and underground cisterns, which were used to collect rainwater for the castle's inhabitants.

In addition to its historical and natural attractions, Antiparos is also home to some beautiful beaches.

The most famous of these is probably Soros Beach, which is located on the south side of the island and boasts crystal-clear waters and fine white sand. Other popular beaches on Antiparos include Agios Georgios, Psaraliki, and Faneromeni Beach.

There are several charming traditional villages on Antiparos that are well worth a visit. The largest and most popular of these is Antiparos Town, which is located on the west coast of the island and boasts a beautiful seafront promenade lined with restaurants, cafes, and bars. The town is also home to the church of Agios Nikolaos, which dates back to the 17th century and features some beautiful frescoes.

Finally, for those who want to explore the surrounding sea, there is a range of activities on offer in Antiparos, including snorkeling, diving, and boat trips to nearby islands. There are also a number of water sports centers where visitors can rent equipment for windsurfing, paddleboarding, and kayaking.

As for accommodation, there is a range of options on Antiparos, from traditional guesthouses and apartments to luxury hotels and villas.

Some of the best places to stay on the island include the Antiparos Hotel, the Hotel Mantalena, and the Aperanto Galazio Villas.

All in all, Antiparos is a beautiful and charming island that is well worth a visit for those looking to explore the Greek islands beyond the more well-known destinations.

Antiparos has recently become a popular celebrity retreat, with notable residents such as Tom Hanks, who owns a villa on the island.

Top Hotels in Antiparos

- ✓ Kouros Village
- ✓ Oliaros Seaside Lodge
- ✓ Artemis Hotel

Chrissi Akti Beach and Nea Chrissi Akti Beach

One of the most beautiful beaches on Paros is Chrissi Akti Beach, also known as Golden Beach. It boasts an extended stretch of fine, velvety sand that shimmers in the sun due to its glassy texture.

Chrissi Akti Beach is especially popular with families with young kids because the water is shallow for a long way out.

The beach is home to numerous beach clubs, tavernas, hotels, and water sports centers that provide lessons and equipment rentals.

While Chrissi Akti Beach, like other Cycladic beaches, is exposed to the strong meltemi winds, its location on the eastern side of the island facing Naxos compresses the wind and increases its intensity, making it the best windsurfing and kitesurfing beach on Paros.

Nea Chrissi Akti Beach (also known as New Golden Beach or Tseredakia Beach), situated about 850 meters north along the coast, hosts the annual Professional Windsurfing World Cup every August, so it is best to make reservations early if you plan to visit during this time.

The Best Hotel at Chrissi Akti Beach

✓ Poseidon of Paros

The Best Hotel on Nea Chrissi Akti Beach.

✓ Acquamarina Resort

Lefkes

Lefkes is a mountain village in central Paros, located in the greenest part of the island, boasting panoramic views of the sea and Naxos island.

It was the island's capital during the medieval era, and its former grandeur is reflected in its 15th-century churches and mix of Venetian, neoclassical, and Cycladic architecture.

The Church of Agia Triada, built in 1830, is its most recognizable landmark, and several smaller churches are scattered around the village.

Once the agricultural hub of Paros, Lefkes is now primarily a tourist destination with wonderful boutiques, tavernas, museums, and galleries.

The Byzantine Road, a popular hiking trail, is an ancient stone footpath dating back to about 1000 A.D. and connects Lefkes with Prodromos village, about 3.5 km away.

Although Lefkes can get crowded, most people do not stay overnight since there are only a few small hotels and guesthouses available.

The Best Hotels in Lefkes

✓ Sweet Path Villa
✓ Agiasi Villas
✓ Villa Byzantino

Fishing Villages

To get a taste of the local life, you can stay in one of Paros' fishing villages, such as Piso Livadi, Ambelas, Aliki, and Drios.

All of these villages have beautiful, sandy beaches for swimming, casual seafood tavernas along the waterfront (many owned by the fishermen's families), and small marinas where you can see the local fishers heading out early in the morning to catch the seafood delicacies.

Piso Livadi is the busiest and most charming of these villages, with three lively beaches and a larger marina on the east side. Aliki, in the southwest, is the largest fishing village, perfect for windsurfing during the summer months, with plenty of restaurants, beaches, affordable hotels, a playground, and the Museum of Cycladic Folklore.

Ambelas is a tiny, family-friendly village offering a quiet stay with a shallow, sandy, calm beach, and a convenient location just 3.5 km from Naoussa. Drios, on the south end of the island, is the quietest of the four villages and only gets busy during August for its windsurfing.

The Best Hotels in Piso Livadi

- ✓ Summer Senses Luxury Resort

The Best Hotels in Aliki

- ✓ Parosland Hotel
- ✓ Afrodite Boutique Hotel

The Best Hotels in Ambelas

- ✓ Margarita Studios

The Best Hotels in Drios

- ✓ Blue Waves Suites & Apartments
- ✓ Villa Vanta

CHAPTER 3

Which Is Better Paros or Naxos

Looking to choose between Paros and Naxos for your next vacation?

Paros is a bustling island with two distinct villages to enjoy, lively nightlife, great food, and unique beaches. On the other hand, Naxos is a relaxed island with long sandy beaches, a charming central village, traditional villages to explore, and plenty of hiking trails.

If you have at least five days to spare, consider visiting both as they are only 40 minutes apart by ferry. Either island makes a great complement to a trip to Santorini, while Naxos offers more of a contrast to cosmopolitan Mykonos than Paros.

For sandy beaches, traditional villages, hearty cuisine, natural beauty, historic ruins and churches, and adventurous activities like hiking and sailing, head to Naxos.

Meanwhile, Paros is the perfect choice for boutique shopping, unusual beaches, gourmet restaurants, and beginner hiking, sailing, and romantic getaways.

Weather-wise, there's not much difference between the two islands.

Late May to early October is the best time to visit, with June through September being ideal for swimming and watersports.

April, May, and October are also great months for sightseeing, dining, and nightlife.

If you're interested in exploring both islands, you're in luck. Naxos and Paros are close enough to each other that visiting both is easy and worthwhile.

With small ports and straightforward ferry connections, there are about 8 direct ferries a day in summer between the two islands from 9:30 a.m. to 10:30 p.m.

You can purchase ferry tickets for this route, but advance tickets are usually unnecessary except during July and August.

Travel agencies throughout Greece sell ferry tickets a few days in advance of your trip.

If you're short on time, consider a day trip to either island.

Both offer sightseeing bus tours to the main villages and cultural highlights, while Naxos boasts fantastic boat trips to the harder-to-reach beaches and sea caves.

On the other hand, Paros has boat tours that visit nearby islands like Antiparos and Despotiko.

Which Is Better Paros or Mykonos

It's difficult to say which is better between Paros and Mykonos, as both islands have their own unique features and appeal to different types of travelers.

Paros is known for its laid-back atmosphere, beautiful beaches, charming villages, and traditional Cycladic architecture. It's a great choice for those seeking a more relaxed and authentic Greek island experience.

Paros is also a popular destination for windsurfing and kitesurfing, with the steady winds of the Cyclades making it an ideal spot for these activities.

Mykonos, on the other hand, is known for its glamorous nightlife, upscale restaurants and bars, and lively party scene.

It's a popular destination for young travelers and those looking to see and be seen. Mykonos also boasts stunning beaches, picturesque whitewashed houses, and a bustling harbor.

Ultimately, the choice between Paros and Mykonos depends on your personal preferences and what you're looking for in a vacation.

If you want a more relaxed, traditional experience, Paros may be the better choice.

If you're looking for a lively party scene and upscale amenities, Mykonos may be a better fit.

Which Is Better Paros or Milos

Paros and Milos are two popular Greek islands that are often compared to each other by travelers planning a trip to the Cyclades.

While they share some similarities, there are some key differences that might make one island a better choice for your vacation.

Geography: Paros is located in the central Cyclades and is one of the larger islands in the group. Milos is located in the southwestern part of the Cyclades and is slightly smaller than Paros.

Beaches: Both Paros and Milos have some of the most beautiful beaches in the Cyclades.

In Paros, you can find a mix of sandy and pebble beaches, some of which are organized with beach bars and water sports while others are secluded and unspoiled. Some of the most popular beaches in Paros include Kolymbithres, Golden Beach, and Santa Maria.

Milos has more than 70 beaches, many of which are secluded and can only be accessed by boat or by hiking. The beaches in Milos are known for their unique rock formations, volcanic landscapes, and crystal-clear turquoise waters. Some of the popular beaches in Milos include Sarakiniko, Firiplaka, and Tsigrado.

Activities: Paros has plenty of activities for visitors, including water sports like windsurfing and kiteboarding. The island is also great for hiking, cycling, and exploring charming villages and historical sites.

Visitors can take a boat tour around the island or visit nearby Antiparos, a small island just a short ferry ride away.

Milos is ideal for those looking for a relaxing holiday, where you can spend your days exploring secluded beaches, coves, and natural wonders.

The island is perfect for swimming, sunbathing, and taking boat trips to see the colorful volcanic landscape and crystal-clear waters.

Culture: Paros has a rich cultural heritage, and visitors can explore the island's ancient ruins, museums, and art galleries.

The island is also known for its traditional Cycladic architecture, and the picturesque villages of Naoussa and Lefkes are popular spots to explore.

Milos also has a rich history and cultural heritage, with several museums and ancient sites to visit. Visitors can explore the charming villages and churches, and learn about the island's traditional cuisine and local customs.

Overall, both Paros and Milos are great choices for a Greek island vacation.

Paros is ideal for those who want a mix of activities, culture, and a lively nightlife scene. Milos is perfect for those who want to escape the crowds and relax on secluded beaches while exploring the island's natural beauty.

The choice between the two ultimately depends on your preferences, budget, and travel style.

Which is Better Paros or Santorini?

Paros and Santorini are two of the most popular destinations in Greece. While both have their unique charms, they offer different experiences to travelers.

Here is a detailed comparison of Paros and Santorini to help you decide which one to visit.

Scenery and beaches

Santorini is famous for its stunning volcanic cliffs, caldera views, and picturesque sunsets. The island's beaches are unique and range from black sand to red and white pebble beaches.

Paros, on the other hand, is known for its crystal-clear waters, long sandy beaches, and charming fishing villages.

Nightlife and Entertainment

Santorini is a more upscale destination and offers a more refined nightlife experience, with upscale bars, clubs, and restaurants. Paros, on the other hand, offers a lively and laid-back nightlife scene, with a wide range of bars, clubs, and beach parties.

History and Culture

Santorini is known for its rich history and culture, with ancient ruins and traditional Greek architecture. Paros has a rich cultural heritage as well, with traditional Cycladic architecture and ancient sites such as the Venetian castle and the Panagia Ekatontapiliani church.

Food and Drink

Both Paros and Santorini offer excellent culinary experiences, with fresh seafood, local delicacies, and traditional Greek cuisine. Santorini is famous for its unique volcanic wines, while Paros is known for its white wines and local spirits.

Accommodation and Prices

Santorini is generally considered more upscale and expensive than Paros, with a range of luxury hotels and villas. Paros offers a range of accommodation options, from budget-friendly guesthouses to high-end resorts.

In conclusion, whether you should visit Paros or Santorini depends on your travel preferences.

If you are looking for a more laid-back, beachy vibe with lively nightlife, then Paros may be the perfect destination for you.

If you are interested in experiencing a more upscale and refined vacation with stunning views, then Santorini may be a better fit.

CHAPTER 4

Paros weather by month

Paros has a Mediterranean climate, characterized by mild, wet winters and hot, dry summers. The weather in Paros is relatively consistent throughout the year, making it a popular destination for tourists.

However, there are some differences in temperature and precipitation between the months, which may affect your decision on when to visit.

Here is a breakdown of Paros weather by month:

January: January is the coldest month in Paros, with average high temperatures of around 14°C (57°F) and average low temperatures of around 8°C (46°F).

January is also the wettest month, with an average of 10 rainy days.

February: February is still considered a cold month in Paros, with average high temperatures around 14°C (57°F) and average low temperatures around 8°C (46°F). February receives an average of 8 rainy days.

March: March marks the beginning of spring in Paros. The average high temperature in March is around 16°C (61°F), while the average low temperature is around 10°C (50°F). March receives an average of 7 rainy days.

April: In April, the weather in Paros starts to warm up. Average high temperatures reach around 19°C (66°F), while average low temperatures are around 13°C (55°F). April receives an average of 4 rainy days.

May: May is a great time to visit Paros, as the weather is warm and pleasant without being too hot. Average high temperatures are around 23°C (73°F), while average low temperatures are around 17°C (63°F).

May receive an average of 3 rainy days.

June: June is the beginning of the summer season in Paros, with average high temperatures around 27°C (81°F) and average low temperatures around 21°C (70°F). June receives an average of 1 rainy day.

July: July is one of the hottest months in Paros, with average high temperatures around 29°C (84°F) and average low temperatures around 23°C (73°F). July receives an average of 0 rainy days.

August: August is the peak of the summer season in Paros, with similar temperatures to July. Average high temperatures are around 29°C (84°F), while average low temperatures are around 23°C (73°F). August receives an average of 0 rainy days.

September: September is a popular time to visit Paros, as the weather is still warm and pleasant but not as hot as July and August. Average high temperatures are around 26°C (79°F), while average low temperatures are around 20°C (68°F). September receives an average of 1 rainy day.

October: In October, the weather in Paros starts to cool down. Average high temperatures are around 22°C (72°F), while average low temperatures are around 16°C (61°F). October receives an average of 3 rainy days.

November: November is considered a cold month in Paros, with average high temperatures around 18°C (64°F) and average low temperatures around 12°C (54°F). November receives an average of 8 rainy days.

December: December is the second coldest month in Paros, with average high temperatures of around 15°C (59°F) and average low temperatures of around 9°C (48°F). December receives an average of 10 rainy days.

Overall, Paros has a pleasant climate throughout the year, but the best time to visit depends on your preferences. If you want to avoid crowds and high temperatures, the spring and fall months are good options.

However, if you want to enjoy the beaches and the summer atmosphere, July and August are the best months.

CHAPTER 5

Pacos without Car

With a good public transportation system and plenty of walking and cycling paths, it's possible to see and experience many of the island's top attractions without the need for a car.

Here are some tips for exploring Paros without a car:

Public transportation: Paros has a good bus system that connects the major towns and villages on the island. The bus schedules are frequent and reliable, and the fares are very affordable. You can easily buy bus tickets at the bus station or on board.

Walking: Paros has many charming villages and scenic walking paths that can be explored on foot.

The most popular walking trails are located in the countryside and offer stunning views of the sea and the mountains. Some of the best walking paths include the Byzantine Road, the Lefkes to Prodromos Trail, and the Marathi Marble Quarries Trail.

Cycling: Cycling is a great way to explore Paros and many rental shops on the island offer bikes for hire.

The island has a good network of cycling paths that connect the major towns and villages, and the terrain is generally flat, making it easy to cycle around.

Taxis: Taxis are readily available on Paros and can be a convenient way to get around if you need to travel long distances or if you're in a hurry.

The fares are reasonable, but it's always a good idea to negotiate the price with the driver before starting your journey.

Water taxis: Paros has a few water taxis that can take you to some of the more remote beaches and coves on the island. This can be a fun and unique way to explore the coastline and enjoy some of the island's more secluded spots.

In conclusion, Paros can be easily explored without a car, thanks to its good public transportation system, walking and cycling paths and the availability of taxis and water taxis.

Whether you're interested in exploring charming villages, hiking in the countryside, or lounging on the beach, Paros has something for everyone.

CHAPTER 6

Cuisine

The cuisine of Paros is renowned for its fresh and simple ingredients. With the close proximity to the open sea, the seafood dishes in Paros are plentiful and delicious.

Seafood dishes are abundant on the menus of restaurants throughout Paros and the freshest of ingredients bring about amazing flavors.

There are a variety of seafood dishes in Paros, such as the delightfully salty calamari and the warm, tender octopus. You can also find an array of grilled fish served with traditional Greek sauces and garnishes.

For those looking for a lighter meal, the Greek Salad is a great option; a perfect blend of fresh tomatoes, cucumbers, onions, and olives mixed with olive oil and oregano.

Served with a side of feta cheese and a glass of red vinsanto, the Greek salad is truly scrumptious!

There are also many meat dishes served in Paros. Grilled meats are taken to a whole new level with the addition of traditional

Greek herbs and spices. Souvlaki is a popular dish in Paros; chunks of tender pork or chicken cooked in a clay pot with vegetables and herbs.

The list of dishes cannot be complete without mentioning the delicious Kites, a traditional dish of grilled or fried pita bread topped with cheese or with a choice of minced meat, egg, and vegetables.

Other dishes include Gyros, kleftiko, moussaka, and dolmadakia, all cooked with the freshest ingredients and boasting traditional Greek flavor.

In order to properly enjoy the local cuisine of Paros, there are a few must-try traditional Greek dishes.

Dakos, for one, is made with toasted barley rusks and topped with tomatoes, Feta cheese, and olives. Bouripanikos salad is a special salad that is prepared with juicy tomatoes, parsley, and onions, which are then topped with a creamy feta cheese dressing and olives.

For a sweet ending, try the traditional Greek baklava, which is a pastry filled with nuts and covered in honey and syrup.

Delightful Greek yogurt with a drizzle of honey on the top is also a perfect dessert.

Paros is a great destination to visit and experience the flavors of Greece.

With an abundance of fresh seafood, traditional meats, and veggies, this island offers something special for all palettes.

So why not come and explore the delicious cuisine of Paros?

CHAPTER 7

Tips and Recommendations for Paros Hotels

• Booking.com is recommended as the best website for finding hotels in Paros.

• Paros is a stunning island, only a 2-hour ferry ride from both Santorini and Mykonos, with fantastic beaches, vibrant nightlife, and picturesque white-washed towns. It is a favorite among Greek islands.

• Parikia and Naoussa are two charming towns to stay in Paros, both offering an abundance of restaurants, nightlife, and lovely beaches nearby.

Parikia has more shopping options, while Naoussa has trendier restaurants and atmosphere.

• The Poseidon of Paros Hotel & Spa and the Astir of Paros are the best beach resorts in Paros, while Pension Sofia, Villa Isabella Studios and Suites, and Margarita Studios are the best affordable hotels.

• The top restaurants on the island are Stou Fred in Parikia, Taverna Glafkos, and Yemeni Taverna in Naoussa.

• The top beaches to visit in Paros are Kolymbithres, Chrissi Akti (Golden Beach), and Santa Maria, easily accessible by bus, but renting a car allows for exploring the island more thoroughly in a short time.

• Antiparos is a fantastic side trip or day trip from Paros, with beautiful beaches, food, and small family-owned hotels. To Stathero is the best restaurant in Antiparos and worth the trip over by itself, serving excellent traditional Greek food steps from where the boats from Paros arrive.

Top Hotels

THE SAINT ANDREA SEASIDE RESORT is a refined, upscale hotel with a dazzling pool, elegant Anastasia Restaurant, and spacious 1 and 2-bedroom suites. It is about a 15-minute walk from Naoussa, Piperi Beach, and Piperaki Beach and offers free transfers to Kolymbithres Beach.

THE POSEIDON OF PAROS HOTEL & SPA is a luxurious beachfront hotel with family-friendly facilities, including 2 pools, 2 kids' pools, a playground, babysitting services, and a VW-van-turned-beach-bar.

The restaurant serves a complimentary Greek and American breakfast buffet and creative Greek dishes, including a kids' menu and allergy considerations.

The hotel is on Chrissi Akti Beach, and a car rental is recommended.

THE PARILIO IS AN ALL-SUITE LUXURY HOTEL near Kolymbithres Beach, with a pool and spa. Suites are spacious and designed for two, with private terraces, bespoke furnishings, and Moroccan textiles. The hotel's signature restaurant, Mr. E, serves gourmet Greek-Mediterranean dishes, and the pool bar offers high-quality cocktails, wine, and light bites. Naoussa village is only a 5-minute drive away, and Kolymbithres Beach is just a 15-minute walk.

THE HOTEL SENIA IS A GORGEOUS LUXURY HOTEL in Naoussa, with an excellent restaurant and 2 pools, including a heated infinity pool and a rooftop adults-only pool. Spacious rooms and suites offer private terraces, some with private jacuzzis. The hotel sits above Piperi Beach with its own designated beach lounge space, and the charming Naoussa port and restaurants are only a 5-minute walk away.

THE PALIOMYLOS SPA HOTEL IS AN UPSCALE HOTEL with a sea-view pool, a tranquil full-service spa, and a roof terrace with sunset views.

Rooms and suites include private balconies or direct pool access, with all suites including fully equipped kitchenettes.

The hotel offers an all-day café and snack bar, serving homemade buffet breakfast, light bites, and drinks.

The hotel is just a 5-minute walk to Piperi Beach and an 8-minute walk to the best restaurants in Naoussa.

LILLY RESIDENCE in Naoussa is a luxury hotel that is exclusive for adults only, offering 12 romantic suites with sea views, some with indoor jacuzzis or private outdoor plunge pools.

The hotel has a hydromassage swimming pool that is open until midnight, a chic bar and restaurant that offers a free evening drink, and a complimentary breakfast buffet with an a la carte egg menu. Service is warm and attentive. Lilly is located on a quiet hillside, a 2-minute walk from Agii Anargyri Beach, and a 5-minute walk to the village of Naoussa.

KANALE'S ROOMS AND SUITES in Naoussa is an upscale hotel with a free-form pool and a creative Greek kitchen near Piperi Beach.

All rooms and suites have private terraces, with most having sea views and indoor jacuzzis.

The rooms are relatively small, so it's best to opt for a suite. The Maisonette Suites are the largest at 55 square meters, while the Penthouse Suites are the most luxuriously appointed and have the best views at 38 square meters.

It's located just above Piperi Beach, a 2-minute walk that includes a steep stairway, and approximately a 7-minute walk to Naoussa's best restaurants and the picturesque Old Port.

ASTIR OF PAROS is a seaside luxury resort in Livadia, near Naoussa. It has a pool, a kids' pool, a private beach, and wonderful restaurants. All suites are large and have private terraces.

Rooms and suites are elegantly appointed, with the largest suite sleeping up to 8 guests. Poseidon (Greek-Mediterranean) and Aeolos (Japanese-Chinese) Restaurants offer exceptional dining, complemented by 2 bars and a daily American buffet breakfast by the pool. The resort is located a 20-minute walk from the rocky Kolymbithres Beach and a 6-minute drive from trendy Naoussa village.

MINOIS VILLAGE BOUTIQUE SUITES & SPA is a 5-star, all-suite hotel with a saltwater pool, kids' pool, and holistic spa overlooking Parasporos Beach.

The suites and villas are spacious and sleep up to 6, with private terraces and pillow menus, and most have sea views. Private pools are available in the Eros Suites, and full kitchens are available in the 2-bedroom villas.

The all-day Mediterranean restaurant offers fantastic dining, including a complimentary Greek breakfast buffet, supplemented by the pool bar and the Deck Lounge Bar for sunset wine and cocktails.

It's located above the quiet end of Parasporos Beach, a 5-minute walk away, and offers free shuttle service to Parikia 4 times a day.

STELIA MARE BOUTIQUE HOTEL is a relaxed, luxury hotel with a pool and an attached jacuzzi, a poolside café, and a spa room with a jacuzzi and hammam.

Rooms and suites all offer private terraces, with most having sea views. The largest suites sleep up to 6, and a hearty Greek buffet breakfast is included with all bookings.

The hotel sits just a 2-minute walk from Agii Anargyri Beach and a 7-minute walk to Naoussa and the Old Port.

KALLISTI ROOMS AND APARTMENTS in Naoussa is a friendly boutique hotel located in a quiet neighborhood that offers a sparkling pool, an all-day pool bar, and sea views from most rooms.

The hotel features suites, apartments, and studios, most of which include kitchenettes and can accommodate up to five guests, each with private terraces.

The hotel is situated on a hill on the edge of Naoussa, just a short walk away from wonderful restaurants near the Old Port, Agii Anargyri Beach is an 8-minute walk away, and Piperi Beach is a 15-minute walk away.

ANNA PLATANOU SUITES in Agia Irini Beach offers a luxurious all-suite getaway with a sea-view pool.

The suites are spacious, each with private terraces and indoor or outdoor jacuzzis, and one even has a private pool. The property offers expansive views of Agia Irini Beach and Antiparos Island.

The Pool Bar serves a delicious Greek breakfast buffet each morning and a menu of light meals, snacks, and cocktails throughout the day, with the most ingredients grown in the owners' garden.

Located in a quiet corner of Paro's near the palm-fringed Agia Irini Beach, the hotel is about a 10-minute drive from Parikia, and a car rental is recommended.

KALYPSO HOTEL in Naoussa is a beachfront hotel run by a family that features a spa and lounge. The hotel offers a wide range of rooms, studios, and suites, each with private terraces.

The Superior Rooms and 1-bedroom Executive Suites include outdoor jacuzzis, while Studios offer kitchenettes. Two of the hotel's rooms are accessible by wheelchair. Most bookings come with a complimentary Greek breakfast buffet, and there is a lounge bar that serves light snacks and drinks until early evening. Kalypso Hotel is located on the rocky end of Agii Anargyri Beach, with a row of sunbeds just a few meters from the sandy swimmable beach. The heart of Naoussa village is just an 8-minute walking distance.

MR. AND MRS. WHITE PAROS in Naoussa is a stylish luxury hotel located on the edge of Naoussa, featuring two stellar pools and an all-day restaurant.

The cozy rooms offer two double beds or one super-king bed, each with private balconies or patios. The spacious Residences offer kitchenettes and are ideal for families or groups of four or five.

The restaurant and pool bar serve small menus of light bites throughout the day, and a free American breakfast buffet is served each morning.

The hotel is located about a 10-minute walk to the center of Naoussa and around a 15-minute walk to Agii Anargyri Beach.

PAROSLAND HOTEL in Aliki is an affordable luxury hotel located in Aliki fishing village, featuring a pool, kids' pool, great food, and just a short walk to three gorgeous beaches.

The well-appointed and spacious rooms can comfortably sleep up to four guests while connecting rooms allow for up to six.

All rooms include private balconies and cell phones with unlimited international calling and data. Elaionas, their all-day Greek restaurant, serves delicious food, and breakfast is included for guests.

Drios Beach is home to the *BLUE WAVES SUITES & APARTMENTS,* an affordable boutique hotel offering studio, one-bedroom, and two-bedroom apartments in a peaceful village.

Guests can enjoy fully-equipped kitchenettes and private terraces with stunning sea views, and the largest apartments can accommodate up to six guests.

A complimentary breakfast is served on each room's terrace, and the hotel is located just steps from the beach. Boutari Beach and Chrissi Akti (Golden Beach) are both within walking distance of the hotel.

Ambelas is where you'll find *MARGARITA STUDIOS*, a cheerful and affordable hotel with a pool, a kid's pool, and a casual restaurant.

The suites, apartments, and house can sleep four to six guests, with many featuring private terraces and kitchenettes.

The hotel also offers a cell phone with data and international calling, a laundry room, and cooking lessons at its restaurant, which is part of the Aegean Cuisine Initiative.

Ambelas Beach is just an eight-minute walk away, and Naoussa is an 11-minute drive, though a car is recommended.

ARGONAUTA HOTEL is an affordable, family-run hotel located in Parikia's main square. Rooms and suites can accommodate up to three guests and feature minimalist decor, with some offering balconies overlooking Market Street, the square, or the sea.

The hotel's popular restaurant serves a la carte Greek breakfast and brunch, which can be delivered directly to the rooms.

The hotel is just a three-minute walk to the ferry port and a five-minute walk to Parikia's bars and restaurants.

PENSION SOFIA is a charming inn in Parikia surrounded by well-maintained gardens with an outdoor dining area, playground, and cozy rooms.

Double and triple rooms offer private terraces, original art, and plenty of charm. But what sets this place apart is the incredibly warm and welcoming owners, Sophia and Manolis, who go above and beyond to make their guests feel like family. The inn is located just a short walk from a small beach, the port, and the heart of Parikia.

VILLA ISABELLA is a welcoming, family-owned hotel with seven studios and one suite, many of which feature kitchenettes and full or partial sea views.

Although most rooms are on the small side, the largest superior studio can accommodate up to four guests and offers 40 sqm of space.

The hotel is conveniently located next to the public stairway leading down to Piperi Beach and is less than a five-minute walk to the center of Naoussa village.

Beaches in Paros

Here are some of the most beautiful beaches in Paros and their locations:

Golden Beach: Located on the southeast coast of the island, near the village of Dryos.

Santa Maria Beach: Located on the northern coast of the island, near the village of Naoussa.

Kolymbithres Beach: Located on the northern coast of Paros, near the village of Naoussa.

Pounda Beach: Located on the southwest coast of Paros, near the village of Pounda.

Piso Livadi Beach: Located on the eastern coast of the island, near the village of Piso Livadi.

Faragas Beach: Located on the southern coast of Paros, near the village of Aliki.

Logaras Beach: Located on the southeastern coast of Paros, near the village of Piso Livadi.

Monastiri Beach: Located on the northern coast of Paros, near the village of Naoussa.

Laggeri Beach: Located on the northern coast of Paros, near the village of Naoussa.

Aliki Beach: Located on the southern coast of the island, near the village of Aliki.

These beautiful beaches offer visitors a range of activities, including swimming, sunbathing, water sports, and relaxation.

Each beach has its unique features and charm, and visitors can explore several beaches during their stay in Paros to experience the island's diverse natural beauty.

Family-Friendly Hotels in Paros

Paros is a popular destination for families looking for a relaxing and enjoyable vacation.

Here are the top 5 family-friendly hotels in Paros:

Paros Bay Hotel: This hotel is located near Parasporos Beach and features a large outdoor swimming pool, a children's pool, a playground, and a tennis court.

The hotel also offers family rooms and suites with kitchenettes and balconies or terraces.

Aelia Hospitality: Aelia Hospitality is a collection of family-friendly villas located near the village of Alyki. The villas feature private pools, fully equipped kitchens, and spacious living areas, making them ideal for families. The property also offers a playground and a game room.

Acqua Vatos Paros Hotel: This hotel is located near Livadia Beach and features a swimming pool, a children's pool, a playground, and a game room.

The hotel offers family rooms with balconies or terraces and kitchenettes.

Parilio, a Member of Design Hotels: Parilio is a stylish and luxurious hotel located near Naoussa.

The hotel features a swimming pool, a children's pool, and a playground. The hotel also offers family rooms and suites with balconies or terraces.

Narges Hotel: This hotel is located near Agii Anargyri Beach and features a large outdoor swimming pool, a children's pool, a playground, and a tennis court. The hotel offers family rooms with balconies or terraces and kitchenettes.

These family-friendly hotels in Paros offer a range of amenities and activities for both adults and children, making them perfect for families looking for a memorable vacation.

CHAPTER 8

Paros for Kids

Paros is a beautiful island in Greece that is perfect for kids to explore and learn about. With its stunning beaches, charming villages, and ancient history, Paros has something for everyone in the family. Here are some of the fun and exciting things that kids can enjoy on Paros:

Beaches:

Paros has some of the most beautiful beaches in Greece, with crystal-clear waters and soft, white sand. Kids can spend the day swimming, building sandcastles, and playing in the sun. Some of the best beaches on Paros include Golden Beach, Santa Maria Beach, and Kolymbithres Beach, which has unique rock formations that kids will love to explore.

Villages:

Paros is home to many charming villages that are perfect for kids to explore. Naoussa, with its winding alleys and fishing harbor, is a great place to walk around and discover hidden treasures.

The village of Lefkes, with its traditional architecture and ancient Byzantine paths, is also a must-visit for kids who love history and culture.

History and Culture:

Paros has a rich history and culture that kids will enjoy learning about. The island is known for its ancient marble quarries, where some of the world's most famous statues were created. Kids can visit the Marble Quarries and learn about the marble-making process and the history of the island.

The Monastery of Agios Ioannis Detis is also a great place for kids to explore. The 16th-century monastery is perched high on a hill overlooking the island, and offers spectacular views of the sea and the surrounding countryside.

Kids can walk around the monastery's beautiful gardens and chapels, and learn about the history of the site.

Food:

Greek food is known for its delicious flavors and healthy ingredients, and Paros is no exception.

Kids will love trying traditional Greek dishes like moussaka, souvlaki, and spanakopita. There are also plenty of sweet treats to try, like loukoumades (honey-dipped donuts) and baklava.

Paros is a great place for kids to learn about Greek history and culture, enjoy the sun and sand, and try delicious food.

Whether you're exploring the island's charming villages or relaxing on the beach, there's something for everyone to enjoy on this beautiful island.

CHAPTER 9

<u>Activities and Attractions Available in Paros</u>

Top Two Tours to Enjoy In Paros

1. Experience a Full Day Sailing Cruise in the Small Cyclades Spend a day sailing through the Aegean Sea and indulge in activities such as snorkeling, sunbathing, and even learning the basics of sailing. Although the exact itinerary is subject to change based on the weather, you will have the opportunity to explore a WWII plane wreck in Iraklia and swim in the waters around Schinoussa, Koufonisia, Naxos, Antiparos, or Despotiko Islands.

You will also be served a traditional Greek lunch with wine included. The departure point is Piso Livadi.

2. Discover Delos and Mykonos with a Full Day Boat Trip Take a full-day excursion to explore Delos and Mykonos on your own. Begin your morning in Delos, the ancient mythological birthplace of Apollo and Artemis and one of the most significant archaeological sites in Greece.

It is highly recommended to hire a guide or join a small group tour upon arrival at the entrance.

In the afternoon, you will have approximately 3 hours to discover the charms of Mykonos on your own.

Take a stroll, sample local snacks, and shop in the delightful alleys of Little Venice, the Old Port, and the Kato Mili windmills.

The Top Things to Do In Paros

PAROS PARK is an expansive 800-acre park located at the northwestern tip of the island, boasting a variety of attractions such as hiking trails, rocky terrain, beaches both secluded and lively, a historic monastery now converted into a cartography museum, an ancient amphitheater used for festivals and events, a picturesque lighthouse, and an open-air cinema that shows movies starting at 9:00 p.m., free of charge.

The park is open 24/7 throughout the year and is accessible by car, water taxi from Naoussa port, or by bus, with a bus stop located about 30 minutes away from Kolymbithres Beach.

KOLYMBITHRES BEACH renowned for its unique moon-like granite rock formations is situated in a bay that faces southeast.

This natural wonder is divided into two main beaches, each with beach clubs offering sunbeds and umbrellas for rent, and further separated into smaller sections by the rocks, providing the opportunity to claim your private beach if you arrive before the crowds.

At the southern end of the beach, a sailing center offers windsurfing and small sailboat rentals and lessons, while kayaks and SUPs can be rented further north.

Access to Kolymbithres Beach can be gained by car, bus, or water taxi ride from Naoussa's Old Port.

THE CHURCH OF PANAGIA EKATONTAPILIANI

or the Church of 100 Doors is one of the most significant churches in Greece, dating back to the 4th century A.D. St. Helene is believed to have founded the original chapel, which was later expanded into a larger church and monastery by her son, Emperor Constantine. Emperor Justinian added a dome to the church in the 6th century.

The complex is well-maintained, and its architecture and artwork exhibit Paleochristian, Byzantine, and post-Byzantine influences, with construction materials from the ruins of older temples.

A small Byzantine Museum of Paros is located within the complex, exhibiting rare icons, relics, and ecclesiastical items, mostly from the 17th and 18th centuries.

The church is located in Parikia, a three-minute walk southeast of the ferry port and five minutes away from the Parikia bus stop.

THE CHARMING VILLAGE OF NAOUSSA is a walkable space that combines Cycladic tradition with worldly sophistication, featuring natural bay beaches, a half-sunken Venetian castle, top-tier restaurants, stylish cocktail bars, all-night dance clubs, luxury boutiques, a winery, and picturesque, domed churches.

Three swimmable beaches (Piperaki, Piperi, and Agii Anargyrii) sit on either side of the port, where fishing boats bob in the sea.

Despite its glamorous and international reputation, Naoussa has preserved its Greek identity, as it is a popular vacation destination for Athenians.

The village is located on the north side of the island, approximately 9 km from the ferry port in Parikia (less than 20 minutes by bus) and about 20 km from the airport.

PARIKIA the capital and largest village on Paros, is where most visitors arrive and depart from the ferry port. As the main harbor and commercial hub over the centuries, it is home to many of the island's significant landmarks, including Panagia Ekatontapiliani, the Frankish Castle ruins, and the Archaeological Museum, as well as amazing restaurants, craft workshops, boutiques, and lively bars, many of which offer sunset views over the sea.

KALOGEROS BEACH is a beach on Paros' east coast, with sand and pebble shores, and crystal blue water, and is set in a small cove below towering rocks.

The beach has a special feature, which is the softening and exfoliating properties of the grey cliffs that are made of unique clay.

By mixing the clay with seawater to create mud, visitors can apply it on their skin to get super smooth skin. Molos Beach is only a 5-minute walk north and is a more traditional beach with sandier shores. Kalogeros is an unorganized beach with no sunbed rentals or restaurants, so visitors need to bring their snacks and gear.

Visitors can plan on driving or taking bus #1 or #5 to Marmara, Marpissa, or Piso Livadi, and walking for 30 minutes to the beach.

NAXOS the largest Cycladic Island, is located only 40 minutes away by ferry and is a sharp contrast to the cosmopolitan atmosphere of Paros.

Visitors can explore the island and find many things to do such as visiting farms, dairies, olive groves, ancient ruins, and marble quarries.

Naxos is home to more than 200 Byzantine churches, connected by hiking trails, with many traditional villages scattered throughout its mountainous interior.

The coastline of Naxos is dotted with sandy beaches that are ideal for fresh seafood tavernas.

The main village of Naxos Town, which has boutiques, bars, and tavernas, is built in the shape of a maze at the base of a 13th-century Venetian castle.

Visitors can take in the stunning sunset sea views over the marina and temple from the many rooftop or balcony restaurants or bars that overlook the charming port.

NAOUSSA'S OLD PORT is the village's main attraction, situated in a picturesque natural bay with fishing boats docked in the marinas and a wide esplanade lined with open-air restaurants and cafes.

The partially submerged Venetian castle ruins, built as a fortress in the 14th century with two watchtowers added in the 15th century, are located at the easternmost tip of the port.

Visitors can take a water taxi from the Old Port that runs to Kolymbithres Beach, Paros Park/Monastiri Beach, and Laggeri Beach.

Water taxis run approximately every hour from 10:30 a.m. to 4:00 p.m. during the summer.

LEFKES is a beautiful mountain village, the highest elevated one in the most fertile part of Paros.

The village boasts panoramic views over the land, sea, and nearby Naxos Island, with its ancient preserved stone pathway, the Byzantine Road, dating back to 1000 A.D. that connects it to Prodromos village and the busy port of Piso Livadi.

This popular hike takes about 90 minutes to the sea one way or about 2 hours to Prodromos and back.

During the Middle Ages, Lefkes was the island's capital and the richest village, with echoes of its past seen in its architecture, including Venetian, neoclassical, and Cycladic buildings that date back to the 15th through the 17th centuries.

The Church of Agia Triada (Holy Trinity), built-in 1830, towers over the village and is the most popular sight. Visitors can reach Lefkes by bus, either by taking the #1 from Parikia or the #5 from Naoussa to Prodromos and then hiking the 3.5 km up or by car.

MORAITIS WINERY which has been family-owned and operated for over 100 years, is the leading winemaker in Paros, with over 100 acres of vineyards spread across the island.

The winery was renovated on top of the original 1910 cellar, where barrels are still aged. Assyrtiko, Mandilaria, Monemvasia, and rare Paro's grape strains are among the varieties.

The winery is open for tastings and self-guided tours from 10:00 a.m. to 4:00 p.m. six days a week. Moraitis is a 10-minute walk from the bus stop and a 5-minute walk from Agii Anargyrii Beach in Naoussa.

WINDSURFING AND KITESURFING: Paros, like most Cycladic islands, receives strong meltemi winds from the north, but its proximity to Naxos island amplifies these winds, making this one of the best windsurfing and kitesurfing spots in the world.

The best windsurfing beaches on Paros are on the island's southeast coast, particularly Chrissi Akti (Golden Beach) and Nea Chrissi Akti (New Golden Beach, pictured above).

Water sports centers with equipment rentals and lessons are available at both of these sandy beaches, as are dive centers, beach clubs, and delicious tavernas.

ANTIPAROS DAY TRIP: Antiparos Island, easily accessible from Paros by car or ferry, is ideal for a day trip. Antiparos' traditional villages, charming marinas filled with fishing boats, idyllic beaches, and authentic Greek tavernas provide a relaxed atmosphere.

Ferries from Paros arrive at Antiparos Town's harbor, with its whitewashed, blocky houses and bougainvillea-lined pathways.

The ruins of a 15th-century Venetian castle, built to defend the island from pirates, are only a few steps from the port (very little of the castle remains intact).

Visitors can walk to 5 wonderful beaches within 5 to 15 minutes from the port or castle (1 with a beach club, 3 with nearby tavernas, and 1 secluded nude beach with no amenities).

The best beaches, however, are further south at Soros (on the way, see the Cave of Antiparos, which has stalagmites and stalactites) and Saint George, which has sunset views.

If you're coming in or out of the port, stop at To Stathero, the best seafood restaurant on the island.

From Paros to Antiparos, there are two ferry options: One option is a 10-minute ride on a car/passenger ferry from the small port of Pounta on Paros' west coast, which is accessible by bus from Parikia.

The second option is a slightly longer boat ride on the passenger-only ferry from Parikia, which runs less frequently - frequently departing just after another ferry arrives - but from the more popular and easily accessible port town.

SANTA MARIA BEACH: The most famous beaches on Paros are known for their stunning scenery and unusual features, but Santa Maria Beach is the best all-around for its simplicity: a long, wide stretch of soft, golden-white sand, fantastic swimming in the calm, clear, aquamarine water, and views of Naxos island to the east.

Swimming, snorkeling, diving, and windsurfing are all available, as are laid-back beach clubs and delectable tavernas.

The north end of the beach has the most amenities, while the south end is quieter. On windy days, head 1.5 km north to Mikri Santa Maria Beach (Little Santa Maria), a protected cove facing south and sheltered from the breeze.

Mikri Santa Maria is home to a dive center, a beach club with sunbed and umbrella rentals, and two charming tavernas.

FISHING COMMUNITIES: Visit one of the island's fishing villages for a taste of local life, relaxing beaches, and delicious seafood. Aliki and Piso Livadi are the most endearing. Aliki is the largest fishing village, with three small beaches (Aliki Beach in the center behind the marina, Piso Aliki outside the marina to the east, and Agios Nikolaos in the bay to the west).

Aliki is a popular destination for families, with a playground, some windsurfing, and the tiny Museum of Cycladic Folklore, which features handmade replicas of traditional boats.

Piso Livadi is a historic port town with a bustling marina full of fishing boats, small ferries, and day cruise pleasure boats. The marina next to the main Piso Livadi Beach has a strip of amazing restaurants and bars; every restaurant is great here, and they are all owned by local fishermen. South of the marina, there are two more beaches: the laid-back Logaras Beach and the trendy Punda Beach.

PAROS ARCHAEOLOGICAL MUSEUM: Excellent museum with indoor and outdoor exhibits of island artifacts, statues, and sarcophagi.

The museum, which was founded to house the findings from the nearby Church of Panagia Ekatontapiliai, is now filled with antiquities dating back to the Neolithic era and including Mycenaean, Hellenistic, Roman, and Byzantine art. The most important works here include the 6th-century B.C. marble Gorgon statue, the 5th-century B.C. colossal marble statue of Artemis, and the 8th-century B.C. Greek statue of a seated figure.

The museum is open daily (except Tuesdays) from 8:30 a.m. to 3:30 p.m. all year. The admission fee is just €2.

PAROS NIGHTLIFE: Whether you're looking for romantic sunsets, all-night dancing, or trendy cocktails, Paros has excellent nightlife for you.

The vast majority of the island's bars and clubs are concentrated in Parikia and Naoussa, with a few beach parties and casual bars open late in the fishing villages. Naoussa is the main nightlife destination, with sophisticated cocktail bars overlooking the waterfront and Old Port, as well as lively dance clubs and after-party spots in the village center. Fotis All Day Bar, Kosmos, and Sommaripa Consolato are among the best bars in Naoussa. Parikia's nightlife scene is more relaxed than that of Naoussa, with a string of rooftop bars offering direct sunset sea views and small bars inside the village with live bands.

Bebop Pirate Bar and Sativa Music Bar are among the best bars in Parikia.

PAROS DINING: Numerous restaurants on Paros serve fresh-caught seafood, hearty Greek comfort foods, and contemporary haute cuisine. Gouna (sun-dried mackerel), mizithra (white goat cheese), and kakavia are some local delicacies (fish and veggie soup).

A few vineyards produce red and white wines, while souma, a grape-based distillate, is the local spirit. Taverna Glafkos and Yemeni in Naoussa, as well as Stou Fred and Ela in Parikia, are among the best restaurants on the island.

BUTTERFLIES VALLEY: A visit to Butterflies Valley is a pleasant diversion on the way to or from the Antiparos ferry. There are no butterflies here, despite the name.

The Jersey Tiger Moth, a daytime moth that appears on the island in June and disappears in August, lives in this green oasis.

The forewings of these small moths are black and white striped, and the back wings are brilliant orange. Outside of the moth season, the park provides a pleasant, shady respite from the day's heat.

The park is open from 9:00 a.m. to 8:00 p.m. from June to September, with an entrance fee of €2.50. It is approximately 5.5 kilometers from Parikia and 4.5 kilometers from the Pounta port.

CHAPTER 10

Answers to Frequently Asked Questions

Where is Paros located?

Paros is an island in the Aegean Sea and part of the Cycladic group in Greece.

It is situated approximately 40 km south of Mykonos, 180 km southeast of Athens, 85 km north of Santorini, and 200 km north of Crete.

How big is Paros?

Paros has a land area of 196 sq. km, which is over three times the size of Manhattan. The island is approximately 22 km in length and 13 km at its widest point.

Its population is around 12,500, and it takes around 30 minutes to drive the longest way from one end of the island to the other.

What is the history of Paros?

A: Paros was first inhabited around 3200 B.C. and later settled by the Cretans, who named it Minoa.

The Minoans and Mycenaeans were the island's primary occupants until the Ionians conquered it around 1100 B.C. The island was later conquered by the Arcadians, followed by the Persians, Athenians, Spartans, Macedonians, Ptolemies, and Romans.

It was also ruled by the Byzantine Empire, and during that era, many churches were constructed, including Panagia Ekatontapiliani.

Paros became a pirate stronghold around the 8th century A.D., and the Venetians ruled the island in the 13th century as part of the Duchy of the Aegean.

The Ottomans conquered it in the early 16th century, and Paros became part of newly independent Greece in 1832.

When is the best time to visit Paros

A: Paros is best visited from late June through early September for warm weather, great swimming, sunbathing, sailing, and nightlife.

If swimming and hot weather aren't your things, the months of April, May, and October are ideal for sightseeing, dining, and shopping.

Most hotels in Paros are open from late April to mid-October.

How can you get to Paros?

You can get to Paros by Greek ferry or direct flights from Athens and Thessaloniki offered by Sky Express and Olympic Air.

Ferries from Athens to Paros make several stops and take anywhere from 3 to 6 hours.

Paros is also connected by direct ferry to Naxos, Mykonos, Ios, Milos, Folegandros, Santorini, and Crete, with many stops along the way.

What are the main towns in Paros?

The two main villages in Paros are Parikia in the west and Naoussa in the north. Parikia is the capital and home to the historic Panagia Ekatontapiliani, the Frankish Castle, the Paros Archaeological Museum, several restaurants, bars, artisan workshops, and boutiques. Naoussa is Paros' most cosmopolitan village, with several fine dining restaurants, high-end cocktail bars, dance clubs, boutiques, and a winery.

Other villages include traditional Lefkes, which was the former capital of the municipality Iria.

Is Paros Expensive?

The truth is, Paros is not the most expensive island in Greece, but it's not the cheapest either. The cost of your trip will depend on several factors, such as the time of year you visit, your travel style, and your budget.

Accommodation is one of the biggest expenses when traveling, and the prices can vary depending on the type of accommodation you choose.

Paros offers a variety of accommodation options, from budget-friendly hostels and guesthouses to luxury hotels and villas. During the high season, the prices tend to go up, so if you're traveling on a tight budget, it's recommended to book in advance and look for deals.

Food and drinks are also an important expense, but in Paros, you can find both expensive and cheap options. Eating at a traditional Greek taverna can be affordable, and you can enjoy delicious food made with fresh local ingredients.

On the other hand, eating at a high-end restaurant or a beach bar can be more expensive.

Transportation is another expense to consider when traveling to Paros. You can rent a car or a scooter to explore the island, but the cost can vary depending on the rental agency and the season. Public transportation is also available, with buses running regularly between the main towns and beaches.

Although the island boasts several luxury hotels, most accommodations in Paros fall into the mid-range category.

Hotels in Parikia are generally less expensive than those in Naoussa.

Budget hotels are typically farther from the water, but there are many affordable options in quieter areas, such as Ambelas or Drios Beaches.

There are no all-inclusive hotels or vacation packages available.

All beaches are public and free to visit, with most beach clubs offering free umbrellas and sunbeds to customers who purchase food or drinks. The ones that charge typically only ask for €10 to €20.

Overall, Paros can be affordable or expensive, depending on your travel style and budget. But even on a tight budget, you can still enjoy the island's beauty and charm, and experience its local culture and hospitality.

With a little bit of planning and research, you can have a memorable trip to Paros without breaking the bank.

Why Travel To Paros?

Paros, one of the many Cycladic islands in Greece, has a lot to offer to all types of travelers.

Here are some reasons why you should consider traveling to Paros:

Beautiful Beaches: Paros has some of the most beautiful beaches in Greece, offering crystal-clear waters and white sand. Kolymbithres Beach, Golden Beach, and Santa Maria Beach are just a few examples of the stunning beaches on the island.

Water Sports: If you are a water sports enthusiast, Paros is the perfect destination for you. The island offers a range of water sports, such as windsurfing, kitesurfing, and diving, making it an ideal spot for adventurous travelers.

Scenic Villages: Paros is home to many scenic and charming villages that are perfect for exploring.

Naoussa, Parikia, and Lefkes are some of the most popular villages, each with its own unique character and charm.

Delicious Cuisine: Paros is famous for its delicious cuisine, which features fresh seafood, locally sourced vegetables, and meats. You can indulge in traditional Greek dishes such as moussaka, souvlaki, and fresh fish.

Rich History: Paros has a rich history and culture that dates back to ancient times. The island has a number of archaeological sites, museums, and monuments that are worth visiting, including the Panagia Ekatontapiliani church and the ancient marble quarries.

Nightlife: Paros has a bustling nightlife scene, with a variety of bars, clubs, and music venues to choose from. Naoussa is known for its lively nightlife, with many bars and clubs staying open late into the night.

Convenient Location: Paros is conveniently located in the heart of the Cyclades, making it an ideal base for exploring other nearby islands such as Mykonos, Santorini, and Naxos.

Overall, Paros is a destination that has something to offer everyone.

Whether you are looking for a relaxing beach vacation or an adventurous water sports trip, Paros has it all. Its beautiful beaches, charming villages, delicious cuisine, and rich history make it a perfect destination for your next vacation.

Is Paros A Party Island?

Paros is not known for being a party island like its neighboring island, Mykonos.

While it does have some nightlife options, they tend to be more low-key and cater to a slightly older and more sophisticated crowd. Naoussa, the main town on the island, has a variety of bars and tavernas that stay open late, but the atmosphere is generally more laid-back than the party scene in Mykonos.

That being said, Paros does have a few places that are popular with younger crowds, such as the Punda Beach Club and Guapaloca Beach Bar, both of which offer music, dancing, and a party atmosphere. These venues are located on the south side of the island, away from the main towns, so they don't disturb the tranquility of the island.

Overall, while Paros does have some nightlife options, it's not a party island like Mykonos. The atmosphere is generally more low-key and relaxed, and the island is more suited to travelers who are looking for a peaceful and authentic Greek island experience.

Can You Fly To Paros from UK

Yes, you can fly to Paros from the UK, but there are no direct flights. You will need to take a connecting flight from Athens, which is the main airport in Greece, to Paros.

There are several airlines that operate flights between Athens and Paros, including Olympic Air and Sky Express.

The flight from Athens to Paros takes around 30 minutes, and there are several flights per day during the summer months. Some airlines may reduce their frequency during the winter months, so it's best to check the schedules in advance.

In addition to flights, there are also ferry services that operate between Athens and Paros.

These ferries run year-round, and the journey takes around 4-5 hours. The ferry ride can be a great way to see the Greek islands, but it may not be the best option if you're short on time.

Overall, while there are no direct flights from the UK to Paros, it's easy to reach the island by taking a connecting flight from Athens or a ferry from Piraeus, the main port of Athens.

What are some of the top beaches in Paros?

Paros has a variety of beaches that cater to different preferences. Santa Maria Beach is considered the best all-around beach, while Kolymbithres stands out for its unique rock formations. Chrissi Akti is ideal for windsurfing or kitesurfing, and Kalogeros Beach features natural mud for a DIY spa day.

All of the beaches are easily accessible by bus, with a water taxi connecting Naoussa to three popular beaches on the north coast.

How Many Days Should I Spend In Paros?

It is recommended to stay for a minimum of 2 nights and 1 full day, but 4 to 7 days would allow for more exploration of the island.

Some suggested activities include hiking in Paros Park, visiting unique beaches like Kolymbithres and Kalogeros, taking a boat tour to swim or snorkel in sea caves, and exploring nearby islands like Antiparos and Naxos.

It is also recommended to take the time to get lost in the charming streets of Parikia and Naoussa and visit their historic sites, restaurants, and shops.

How can I get around Paros?

The island's public bus system is an easy way to get around Paros, with fares varying by route and distance traveled.

Renting a car is another option for more flexibility, as the roads are in good condition and easy to navigate.

Pre-arranged transfers provided by hotels or services like Welcome Pickups can also be arranged from the Naxos airport or ferry port to your hotel.

How Do I Get To Antiparos?

Antiparos is a great day trip or overnight destination from Paros, located directly to the west of it. Regular car-commuter boats run from the small port of Pounta, accessible via bus or taxi from Parikia Port, from early morning to midnight.

During the summer, there are also frequent passenger-only ferries departing directly from Parikia Port, and Antiparos has excellent beaches, restaurants, and small family-owned hotels.

Many well-known American celebrities frequent the island, so if you make a day trip, be sure to eat at To Stathero, the island's finest restaurant.

Currency Used In Paros?

The Euro (€) is the currency used in Paros and all over Greece. In Parikia, Most shops, bars, and restaurants in Naoussa and the island's main beaches accept credit cards, with a minimum purchase required.

Otherwise, there are plenty of ATMs nearby. It's a good idea to have some cash on hand for small purchases and bus trips.

There are far fewer ATMs and more cash-only businesses in the smaller villages.

Is Paros Good For Families

Yes, Paros is a great destination for families, thanks to its beautiful beaches, family-friendly attractions, and safe, welcoming environment.

Here are some of the reasons why Paros is a good choice for families:

Beaches: Paros is home to many beautiful beaches that are ideal for families. Some of the best family-friendly beaches include Golden Beach, Santa Maria Beach, and Livadia Beach, which offer calm waters and plenty of space for children to play.

Water sports: Paros is a popular destination for water sports, and many of the island's beaches offer opportunities for families to try activities such as windsurfing, kayaking, and paddleboarding. There are also several dive centers on the island, which offer introductory scuba lessons for children.

Activities: Paros offers plenty of family-friendly activities beyond the beaches. Families can explore the island's ancient sites and museums, take a boat tour around the island, or visit the Butterfly Valley nature reserve.

Safe environment: Paros is a safe and welcoming destination, with a low crime rate and friendly locals who are used to welcoming families. The island is also easy to navigate, with good infrastructure and reliable transportation options.

Accommodation: Paros offers a range of family-friendly accommodation options, including hotels, apartments, and villas. Many of these properties are located close to the beach or other family-friendly attractions.

Overall, Paros is a great destination for families, with plenty of activities and attractions to keep children of all ages entertained. The island's safe environment and family-friendly infrastructure make it a great choice for a relaxing and enjoyable family vacation.

Glossary

Aegean Sea – A vast body of water lying between the Greek mainland and the islands of the eastern Mediterranean.

Airport – An area dedicated to the transport of passengers, cargo, and mail either by plane or boat.

Archaeological Site – A place where remains of ancient civilizations are found. These sites include monuments, buildings, and artifacts.

Beaches – A shoreline of land usually sandy or covered with pebbles, ideal for swimming and sunbathing.

Bicycle – A two-wheeled vehicle designed for transportation.

Cuisine – The style of cooking and the foods associated with a particular region or culture.

Fishing – The practice or activity of catching or harvesting fish for food and/or recreation.

Golden Beach – A beautiful beach located on the south coast of Paros measuring approximately 3 kilometers.

Hiking – The activity of walking or climbing outdoors, either by oneself or with a group, usually on designated trails or paths.

Island – A piece of land that is surrounded by water on all sides, usually with no mainland connection.

Kitesurfing – A water sport combining elements of kite flying and surfboarding that is growing in popularity around Paros.

Livadi – A fishing village located on the south coast of Paros, known for its traditional restaurants and taverns.

Monastiri – An ancient fortified monastery located on the south end of Paros, built by the Venetians.

Naoussa – A picturesque fishing village on the northwest coast of the island, known for its preserved buildings, vibrant nightlife, and local restaurants.

Parikia – The main town and port of Paros, located on the western coast of the island.

Relaxation – The act of resting, calming down, and reducing stress in a peaceful environment.

Sailing – The practice of navigating a boat through the open seas using the power of the wind.

Taxi – A car or carriage used for hire to transport passengers from one place to another.

Village – A small settlement typically consisting of a few houses and shops, found in rural areas.

Watersports – Any recreational activity taking place in the water e.g. swimming, diving, surfing, sailing, waterskiing, etc.

Printed in Great Britain
by Amazon

23974532R00086